MW00366378

On FRAGILE WINGS

Stories of Hope from the Inner City

DOUG FORSBERG

A FOUR-WEEK DEVOTIONAL

NAZARENE INDIAN BIBLE COLLEGE
2315 MARKHAM RD. S.W.
ALBUQUERQUE, NM 87105

BEACON HILL PRESS OF KANSAS CITY
Kansas City, Missouri

20045

Copyright 1995
by Beacon Hill Press of Kansas City

ISBN 083-411-5530

Printed in the
United States of America

Cover design: Crandall Vail and Mike Walsh

All Scripture quotations not otherwise designated are from the *Holy Bible, New International Version®* (NIV®). Copyright © 1973, 1978, 1984 by International Bible Society. Used by permission of Zondervan Publishing House. All rights reserved.

Permission to quote from other copyrighted versions of the Bible is acknowledged with appreciation:

The *New American Standard Bible* (NASB), © 1960, 1962, 1963, 1968, 1971, 1972, 1973, 1975, 1977 by The Lockman Foundation.

The *New King James Version* (NKJV). Copyright © 1979, 1980, 1982, Thomas Nelson, Inc.

Scripture quotations marked KJV are from the King James Version.

10   9   8   7   6   5   4   3   2   1

For DeVonna

Compassionate minister
Loving wife
Faithful friend

Contents

Acknowledgments

I would first like to express my deepest gratitude to Gene Fuller, who served as my district superintendent during my years of ministry in Fort Worth and St. Petersburg, Florida. Our ministry was made possible by the support and encouragement given to us by Dr. Fuller and his wife, Evelyn.

My dear friend and professor Albert Truesdale must be mentioned for the quality of his teaching and the guidance he provides for his students. How fortunate I was to be numbered among them!

My parents, Dwayne and Inez Forsberg, also played a vital role in the development of our ministry and in the writing of this book with their love, their wisdom, and their willingness to pay exorbitant telephone bills.

No expression of appreciation would be complete without mentioning my wife, DeVonna. Her depth of devotion to Christ and her impassioned love for children have touched all who know her. She has faithfully served with dignity, strength, compassion, and a joyful, sweet spirit that is unsurpassed. The children mentioned in this book and the one who wrote this book will forever be in her debt.

Introduction

"You feel called to *where?*" This question that my mother asked me in the fall of 1983 became one I would have to answer many times in the days and months that followed. During that unforgettable fall, while a student at Nazarene Theological Seminary in Kansas City, I began to sense God drawing me to a very unfamiliar place. God had led me to an intersection in my spiritual journey, and all roads were closed with the exception of one—the road that led to the inner city.

In 1983 I began to prepare for urban ministry, and since my graduation in 1985 I have faced situations and experiences most Americans only read about or see on television news programs. The tragedy of inner-urban areas is often difficult to comprehend. Who in his or her right mind would wish to confront drug abuse, domestic violence, child abuse, homelessness, crime, or human despair? City officials, politicians, and church leaders often cite answers to the problems and create strong proposals for inner-city healing. The trouble has always been finding the right people to deliver the message and administer the healing. A key question is "Who will go for us?" (Isa. 6:8).

The fact of the matter is—I went. Now, upon reflection, I am glad I did. The lessons I learned were difficult, tragic, and painful. However, in the reflection of those lessons I learned about the Father heart of God, the immediacy of the Holy Spirit, and the healing power of Christ—all very precious to me.

This book is an attempt to share with you some very valuable lessons I learned. The lessons are taken mostly from my experiences as an urban pastor in the Dallas-Fort Worth area and the St. Petersburg, Florida, area. Some lessons are taken from my childhood with an eye toward the future and the man I would become.

I do not write in order to heap guilt upon my readers for

not being inner-city heroes, nor do I write to inflate my importance as an inner-city pastor above the suburban pastor or rural pastor who also obeyed a call of God. I merely pass the lessons along in the hope that through them you will make some wonderful discoveries about yourself, about God, and about the love He desires to infuse into all human life. Most important, I wish for you to discover that, despite what you read in the paper or view on television, there is hope—and much hope at that!

1 On the Banks of the Hope-Again Stream

There I will give her back her vineyards, and will make the Valley of Achor a door of hope. —HOS. 2:15

About one mile south of Jericho lies a valley called Achor. The valley got its name, which means "trouble," during the days of Joshua, when Achan was punished by death for the crimes he had committed. Since that day the Valley of Achor has come to represent the valley of suffering.

Hosea has become a very cherished book for me. The message of Hosea is simple. Even though God's children played the harlot in loving other gods, He still loved them and longed for them to return. The dramatic message was played out in the life of Hosea when he was commanded of the Lord to marry the prostitute Gomer. It became evident that God was a forgiving and long-suffering lover of His people, as Hosea was a forgiving and long-suffering lover of his unfaithful wife.

In the midst of Hosea's book, we come across the Valley of Achor once again. Israel, of her own volition, had betrayed her loving God and found herself in the valley of suffering. This time, however, there was a door. The door was called "the door of hope."

In my experience as an inner-city pastor, I have personally witnessed the tragic consequences of sin. Many times the affliction was self-induced through alcohol or drug abuse. Other times the affliction fell upon the innocent. I knew from the start I was ministering in the Valley of Achor.

One sunny Saturday morning my wife and I were picking up some children for our Saturday children's activity. One girl we picked up had been abused the night before; the memory of her wounded five-year-old face will stay with me forever. On another occasion while feeding street people in downtown Dallas, I discovered a middle-aged, homeless man having an epileptic seizure on the front lawn of Dallas City Hall. It was 10 P.M., and no one was around to help.

In our modern world many people, including children, live in the valley of suffering. In the inner city—the modern American "Valley of Achor"—the murky tide of despair will sweep away anyone who would try to help unless he or she continually remembers the truth of Hosea. In the Valley of Achor there is always a door of hope.

That door, of course, is Christ. His Spirit, always present, always powerful, and always loving, is the hope of our world. Even though our world's most tragic epidemic is hopelessness, there is an accessible cure.

One night I had a nightmare. In my dream a long line of broken people were walking. Some were elderly. Some were children. All were suffering. Ahead of them was a green valley, and running through the valley was a stream. When I awoke, I contemplated the dream. After a day of thought, I concluded that the valley was Achor and the stream was hope. Before I slept again, I decided to put my dream to verse. I called the poem "The Hope-Again Stream." This stream runs through every valley of suffering and offers to anyone who would drink of it the healing power of hope.

> *Somewhere not so far from here,*
> *Broken hearts and broken dreams*
> *Entwine, planting seeds of hope-again tears*
> *On the banks of that Hope-Again Stream.*
>
> *Nowhere in this world of ours*
> *Is hope grass so velveteen*
> *Or be so many hope-again flowers*
> *Than on banks of that Hope-Again Stream.*
>
> *Someday soon you will find out*
> *What others have found and seen:*
> *The sun coming up through the mist of doubt*
> *On the banks of the Hope-Again Stream.*

Doug Forsberg

₌2 The Unknown Future and the Known God

For I know the plans I have for you. —JER. 29:11

No matter how near we draw to God, we will never know the future. Even if we serve Him with cyclonic energy and search for Him with all our hearts, God remains silent when asked to reveal the future. Our comfort as God's children does not rest in our knowledge of the future, but in our knowledge of God himself.

A few years ago when DeVonna and I were ministering in Fort Worth, I received a phone call at 3 A.M. on a bone-chilling January night. The male voice on the other end was panic-stricken. He was an infrequent attendee of our church who had been thrown into jail earlier that day. His panic was because his two children, ages two and four, had been involved in an auto accident, and he did not know their condition. All he knew was that his roommate had been drinking, took the children in his car, and hit a telephone pole.

I told the man on the phone I would come to the jail, and together we would find out what had happened. I dressed and headed for the jail in the 10-degree darkness.

When I arrived at the jail, the man who had called me was sitting in his cell with his two children on his lap. The children had a few scrapes and cuts, but their father was over-joyed that, for the most part, they were unharmed. The ambu-lance driver had taken the children to the jail, and now the po-lice were in a quandary about what to do with them.

DeVonna and I took temporary custody of those two little ones that cold night. I told their father we would look after them until other arrangements could be made.

One of the police officers and I wrapped the children in some blankets (they had no coats) and carried the shivering little children to my car. As we walked to the parking lot, I couldn't help but think how frightened these two little ones must be. Their father was in jail, they had been in a car accident under the care of a drunk, and now they were going home with a stranger.

What I will always remember from that night was a question the four-year-old girl asked me when I buckled her seat belt in the backseat of my car. As I fastened the buckle, she held my arm and looked up at me with frightened brown eyes and asked, "Can you dwive?"

On that January night a child was struggling with the issue of trust. In my own walk with God, I have come to understand that our fear of the future has at its heart the issue of trust. When once the trust issue is settled, the fear of the future melts away. Those of us who have served God through the years have learned that on cold, dark nights, when the future is uncertain, there is a certainty in the trustworthiness of God.

Maybe God's response to us during our own times of struggle might be similar to what I told a frightened four-year-old little girl on a dark, cold Texas night: "Yes, little one, I can dwive."

14   *Doug Forsberg*

≡3 Homeless Feet and the God Who Cares

Indeed, the very hairs of your head are all numbered.

—LUKE 12:7

The few minutes before a worship service are, more often than not, fairly frantic for a minister—at least they have always been for me. It seems that no matter how prepared you are, there are always last-minute interruptions of various magnitudes.

In my few years of inner-city pastoral ministry, last-minute interruptions prior to the worship service have run the gamut of pastoral nightmares. Now, what seemed to be disasters I can look back upon with a touch of humor. I can remember such last-minute bulletins as "Pastor Doug, the ladies' toilet is overflowing!" or "The teens are in the attic making birdcalls!" Others commonly included "Pastor Doug, there's a dog loose in the sanctuary!" and "The door on the church van just fell off!"

One particular last-minute interruption comes to mind, however, when I am putting on my socks every morning. This interruption came one beautiful spring day when one of our homeless men came into my office one minute before the service began. His middle-aged, careworn face was troubled, and I asked, "Tim, I have only a few minutes, but what can I help you with?"

"I want you to pray for my feet," Tim said. "They are hurtin' an awful lot."

As I further inquired about his condition, he took off his very worn cowboy boots. What I saw nearly made me ill. His feet were literally covered with bleeding blisters. "Don't you have any socks, Tim?"

NAZARENE INDIAN BIBLE COLLEGE
2315 MARKHAM RD. S.W.
ALBUQUERQUE, NM 87105

"No," he replied, as though I had asked him a dumb question.

A few minutes later I entered the sanctuary (two minutes late) and stepped to the pulpit to call the congregation to worship. As I did, there were a few things different with me that day. One was that I wasn't wearing any socks. I had given my pair to Tim, along with the promise that after the service we would find him a decent pair of shoes, some more socks, and some medicine for his feet. Another difference was a bit more subtle. I realized that day, through the loss of my socks, that God is a God who cares about socks.

When Jesus told His disciples, "Indeed, the very hairs of your head are all numbered," He was revealing to them a wonderful truth about God's nature, a truth that points to the reality of God's knowing and caring. The reality of an all-knowing God is often a theological given. But to comprehend that, as well as having a universe to run and a race to save, God's caring is as far-reaching as His knowing—well, that's just plain hard to believe. Yet, sitting in my office that day, looking at two bloody and blistered feet, I couldn't help but know that God cared—and cared deeply—about those homeless, sockless feet.

Doug Forsberg

=4 Precious–and Forgotten

*Do not cast me away when I am old; do not forsake me when
my strength is gone.* —PS. 71:9

Weekly I make a trip. This trip isn't to a sporting event, to the
store, or even to a church. It is to the nursing home—a place
where people live their last remaining years eating, sleeping, and
dreaming of days gone by and people they love. And hoping.

Younger generations rarely think about nursing homes or
the people who call them home. In my weekly visits I have discovered that I was the only preacher who provided a worship
service for the dear people I grew to love—and for many I was
their only weekly visitor.

It goes without saying that our society worships youth,
talent, and beauty. People who lack these, especially the elderly, often are discarded and forgotten. Their wisdom and love go
neglected while their perceived worth and value diminish. Few
baby boomers take the time to discover that residing within
the halls of the local "old folks' home" is pure gold that never
will be reported in the *Wall Street Journal* or on the financial
page of the local newspaper. It is the gold of human dignity,
hope, and wisdom—gold waiting to be mined by someone
who has love enough to care.

I grew up learning about life while wedged in a rocking
chair with an old woman. According to our society, her talent-
ed days were over. Her youthful beauty could be seen only in
faded black-and-white pictures on the piano. In her heart,
however, the love she harbored could fill an ocean, and her
wisdom was "from above" (James 3:17, KJV). Always in her
lap was an old, worn, marked-up Bible.

When she died in 1971, a light went out in my heart forever. That corner of darkness in my heart could be lit by no one else but my Grandma Turner. Grandma left me no money, but she left me with treasures worth far more than money.

Each week I make a pilgrimage to a place where someone else's grandma and grandpa live. I listen to them, hold them, love them, sing with them, preach to them, and pray with them. I watch them smile, laugh, cry, dream, hope, remember, and, yes, even die. I deny that it's my gift or calling, because I see it as neither a gift nor a calling. Any who say it is may only be attempting to excuse from biblical commands the many who are following the world's view that old folks aren't worth much and that they surely aren't worth *my* time or effort.

They are worth every minute of our time and every bit of our effort. Perhaps I have added to their lives a little, but they have added to my life a lot. Many times I don't feel like going to the rest home. Every time I am glad I went.

Doug Forsberg

=5 The Day Words Failed

And by his wounds we are healed. —ISA. 53:5

The night I met him he swore at me. I was walking in downtown Dallas with a recent convert when suddenly a man came out of the darkness of a parking garage and confronted us. His jet black hair was long and thick. His eyes were glazed over as if he were chemically dependent. He limped as he walked, and he swore as he spoke.

His anger quickly abated as we offered him food and hot tea with the assurance we were there to help and not to condemn. Tears filled his eyes as he told us his story of nine years on the street after losing his family of four and his well-paying job. That night we mostly listened. He talked for two hours as though he had never had an attentive audience before. We asked if we could drive him anywhere; he requested that we take him to the place where he was staying. It was a stripped-out 1966 Ford Mustang in the central junkyard of Dallas. It had served as his home for the past several months.

I remember "spiritual" discussions with my newfound friend that exposed his belief that God hated him and longed for his destruction. Beyond that, he saw his case as helpless because he had slit both his wrists and given his soul to the devil in a satanic ritual years before. My words of comfort and hope fell like dust to the ground as he held out his arms and exposed his wounds.

Months of praying, helping, listening, and loving resulted in new birth for my friend. It came on the day when he finally realized that the scars on the hands of the Son of God were more redeeming and more powerful than the satanic scars he carried on his wrists. His blood oath to Satan was nullified by the blood-bought purchase of God's only begotten.

The change was subtle but remarkable. His hair was still long, thick, and black. He still limped as he walked. But curses had been turned into blessings, and his eyes sparkled from the inner rays of the light of hope that had begun to shine in his heart.

The story doesn't end here. One year after we met, a Christian television program called me and asked if they could interview my friend and me for their program. Both of us agreed. They decided to tape the interview on the very spot we had met the night he swore at me for being a "Jesus person."

On the day of the taping, we gathered around the entrance to the parking garage across from Dallas City Hall. A crowd of 40 or so curious Dallas businesspeople began to gather as the director gave us our last-minute instructions: "Doug, ask short, simple questions. Dave, give him honest answers in clear sentences—and, by the way, show some emotion as you speak."

After those few instructions, the director signaled to begin rolling. On that most memorable day words failed, but never had there been more clear communication.

I held the microphone in my sweaty hand and spoke into it: "Dave, tell us what your life was like one year ago today, and then tell us what your life is like now."

I then held the mike up to my dear friend's lips. To my astonishment, those lips began to quiver, and big tears began to roll down the face of the man who was to become my greatest inspiration.

"Well . . . ," he said. That was all he said. The tears of joy and wonder overpowered both of us, and we cried like babies in front of bewildered businesspeople in the light of the Texas sun.

Doug Forsberg

=6 The Nameless Shiverer

And he took the children in his arms, put his hands on them and blessed them. —MARK 10:16

It was 20 degrees on the Saturday night before Christmas, and we were feeding approximately 100 street people a barbecue dinner outdoors in a vacant parking lot across from Dallas City Hall. We had a glorious spread of barbecue meats, potato salad, baked beans, and coleslaw, all donated by local barbecue restaurants. The food was plenteous and aromatic as the people with hearty appetites began to assemble before our three long folding tables piled with food. We were to begin serving at 7 P.M.

My job that night was coleslaw. I stood behind a table that held three large aluminum pans piled high with "famous slaw" from various restaurants. I spooned out about 30 pounds of it to the smiling people who filed by that night. Thanks to the 20-degree temperature and the fairly stiff wind, the "famous slaw" stayed fresh the entire duration of our two-hour dinner.

What was to be a joyful and convivial event turned sour for me that night. I was scooping out the slaw from my third tray when I saw her standing at one corner of the parking lot. She was about three years old. She was poorly dressed and was holding hands with a woman whose dress was just as shabby, maybe even more so. What startled me, as I scooped out some slaw and placed it on a plate, was that the little girl was shivering so. Her little body seemed to quake as her big eyes sparkled from the streetlight above.

I decided to walk over to the woman and the child. I walked down the serving line, found someone to take my place at the coleslaw, and then walked over to where the woman and child had been. They were gone. I searched the parking lot and the crowd in vain. I never got to meet that nameless little shiverer. I never got the chance to find her a coat or a place to stay. I never got the chance to take her by the hand and lead her to the warmth of our kerosene stove.

The really strange thing about her is that ever since that day, when my family and I decorate our Christmas tree, I think about that little girl and the thousands like her who brave cold nights with only hope to warm them. Christmas reminds me of her. Cold weather reminds me of her. Yes, even coleslaw reminds me of her.

Last summer my entire family gathered for a giant barbecue. We had a glorious spread of barbecue meats, potato salad, baked beans, and coleslaw. When I was asked to give the blessing, I need not tell you who I thought of—and for whom I prayed.

Doug Forsberg

⹀7 Garbage Truck Home

Foxes have holes and birds of the air have nests, but the Son of Man has no place to lay his head. —MATT. 8:20

I was indoctrinated into the ins and outs of homeless life by a friend who runs a ministry in Dallas. His ministry at that time consisted of a van filled with donated sandwiches and tea. He would drive to seven or so locations each evening, where he fed and ministered to the homeless. The ministry was called Soul Patrol. Mark, the director, was an eccentric fellow, harboring a pure heart of love for those to whom he was called to minister. Mark taught me things and showed me sights that became a second seminary education.

On that first night as I rode with him in the Soul Patrol van, I entered a world as foreign and strange to me as some remote country. Our third stop that night came at about 9 P.M. as we entered the truck junkyard in downtown Dallas. "Don't tell me people live here!" I cried. Mark just laughed at my naïveté.

He gave his usual signal of four toots on the van horn. Emerging from the rusting heaps of metal came people—worn, weary-looking, hungry people. I sat motionless in the van as I counted about 40 men and women who called the truck junkyard home.

Finally regaining my composure, I leaped out of the van and joined Mark in his nightly labor of love of listening to and feeding these wounded journeymen on life's highway. Most were Hispanic and were living in the United States illegally. Some of them held jobs, but none of them had homes.

I returned there many times, and a man named Louis was particularly memorable. I met him during my first visit with

Mark. Louis struggled to communicate with me in broken English mixed with Spanish.

"Louis," Mark shouted, "show Doug your home!" Louis nodded in agreement and led me to his home. It was the back end of a garbage truck. Louis had cleaned it out, and remarkably so. It was a neat, clean, little room with wooden floors, a small bed, a lampstand with a candle, and a picture on the wall. Louis smiled with pride at his humble dwelling and held up three fingers. "Three months I live here," he said as he continued chewing a sandwich with what teeth he had left.

That evening Louis and I talked about his life and life in general. Louis had a faith many would call simple, yet at the same time profound. I had seen faith like his before and would see it again and again as the poor became my friends.

The astonishment of seeing people living in that junkyard has never worn off. Sitting there with Louis in his garbage-truck home is now but a tender memory. The picture Louis had on the wall was of Jesus. Never did a picture of Christ hold such profound meaning for me. The face of Christ on the wall of a garbage truck does not seem strange or out of place.

It was astonishing to find people living in a junkyard. To discover Christ among them was not.

Doug Forsberg

=8 Jesus Is Still a Carpenter

God makes a home for the lonely. —PS. 68:6, NASB

Lessons we learn as children stay with us. My personal belief system and theology were greatly influenced by a dear saint by the name of Mrs. Suffridge. She used to lead the children's church services in my home church in Kansas City. The songs and the stories have remained a strong influence in my life in spite of the fact that I bade farewell to childhood years ago. While others are whistling current pop tunes, sometimes I find myself whistling or singing, "I will make you fishers of men"; or "He's able, He's able, I know He's able"; and even "Stop, and let me tell you what the Lord has done for me."*

One story and song were taught over and over again. The story was that of Jesus and His cross, and the song was "Into My Heart." Mrs. Suffridge told us repeatedly that Jesus wanted to build a home in our hearts. Only when we asked Jesus into our hearts would we ever find salvation, joy, and life itself. One Sunday, Mrs. Suffridge asked if any of us would like to ask Jesus to come into our hearts to live. On that day, I asked Jesus to come and live in my heart. He did and I believe He has been there ever since.

The trouble, however, is that Jesus was not satisfied with His home in my heart. During my years in seminary He began to add on rooms. The spiritual banging and sawing and foundation building was difficult for me. Yet Jesus persisted in remodeling His "heart home."

I have since discovered that Jesus, the Carpenter, was adding rooms in my heart for others. He built rooms for chil-

---

*"Stop" © 1963 Child Evangelism Fellowship, Inc. (Administered by The Copyright Co., Nashville, Tenn.) All rights reserved. International copyright secured. Used by permission.

dren, for the poor, for hurting people, and even for sinners. Jesus is not satisfied until you let Him expand your heart to include those for whom He gave His life. Being a Christian is not just asking Jesus into your heart. It also involves giving Him permission to continue to build, expand, and remodel. Jesus is not finished being a carpenter until your "heart home" is as big as the world, and everyone is welcome.

Thirty years ago in the basement of a small church, a dear old saint taught a handful of children that Jesus was a carpenter and that He is the Savior of the world. That Carpenter/Savior is still saving—and building.

=9 From Pastor to Nonperson

Before Philip called you, when you were under the fig tree, I saw you.
—JOHN 1:48, NKJV

A very good friend of mine once accomplished a feat that I had always dreamed of but never quite had the courage to pull off. He became a street person for one night.

My friend prepared by allowing his appearance to resemble that of a man who had been on the street for quite some time. He allowed his beard to grow to stubble length and refrained from his normal routine of hair care. He dressed and acted the part to perfection. This pastor friend of mine, who had never smoked, even went so far as to chomp on one end of an old cigar.

As I remember his appearance, I would be inclined to laugh if not for the fact that behind his costume was the sad reality that thousands of human beings are playing the same part without acting and with little hope of escaping the homeless stage.

It was not funny to us then; it is not funny to us now. We learned some tragic truths.

That one night as a homeless man on the streets of Fort Worth was an invaluable lesson for my friend and me. We both anticipated he would be sneered at and looked down upon. We knew a certain amount of danger was involved, but we never expected the result.

The day following his "homeless night," my friend reported to me his remarkable observation. With concern in his eyes and stubble on his face, he revealed to me the terrible plight of the homeless man: "I became a nonperson. Everywhere I went, it was as if I were invisible. No abuse, no sneering, no harsh remarks—just the uncanny feeling that I had no value or meaning. It was as if I didn't exist at all."

The worst fate that can befall a human being is to become a nonperson in the society in which he or she lives. Hope, encouragement, love, justice, peace, security, belonging, and well-being are things society cannot offer to people it refuses to see.

The night my friend became friendless in Fort Worth brought to life the wonderful meaning of the simple words Christ spoke: "I saw you."

=10 The Palace of Dallas

For the Son of Man has come to seek and to save that which was lost. —LUKE 19:10, NKJV

Many people take great pride in the bars they frequent. Having grown up in the church, it seems odd to me that non-Christians boast about their bars as Christians boast about their churches. In a strange way, a bar can sometimes function as a sanctuary for people who are lost.

I have frequented only one bar during my ministry; that bar no longer exists. It used to be located in central downtown Dallas and was known as the Palace of Dallas. Its half-burned-out, buzzing neon sign would beckon those passing by.

The folklore surrounding this curious place was colorful, to say the least. I always held the legends suspect, but those who frequented the Palace of Dallas believed them to be true. The bar, supposedly the oldest in Texas, was once owned by Jack Ruby. During its heyday it was bustling with all sorts of activity and was always in the center of organized crime, and unorganized crime as well.

I first set foot in the bar on a humid summer evening years after its heyday had passed. Several business owners had informed me that it had become a hangout for street people. It had become a 24-hour sanctuary for lost and homeless people who basically had nowhere else to go. That first night I carried a sack of tuna sandwiches and some flyers about our ministry. I also entered with the assurance that I was "prayed up" and "led" to enter this foreign place.

The door was on street level, but the entrance to the bar was up a flight of stairs. The staircase was dark, and the sound of my pounding heart was drowned out by the creaking of the old wooden stairs. On the way up I met two men coming down; they appeared to be 10 feet tall on the stairs above. Politely, I flattened myself and my tuna sandwiches up against the wall to let them pass. Their black leather jackets and long black beards made them nearly invisible on the dark staircase. After they passed, the staircase smelled of leather, alcohol, and tuna.

At the top of the stairs I entered what was to become a place of cherished memories. The bar was an old, dingy, dirty, smoky, foul-smelling place. But it was full of people who in time would become my friends and would call me "Preacher," "Pastor Doug," or just plain "Rev." What shocked me that night was that they welcomed me. At least they welcomed my sandwiches. I introduced myself to each person, one by one. During my first few hours there, amid the cracking of pool balls and the clinking of beer bottles, I listened to their stories—stories like yours and mine, only more desperate and depraved. That night I met the owner, the bartender, and a few of the regulars. I also learned why the place was special. It was the one place homeless persons could go and feel welcome.

Two years later, the Palace of Dallas and the adjacent buildings were purchased by the power and light company. On that same location today stands a new shopping area complete with fountains and park benches. Homeless people are not welcome.

During those two years, I walked those creaky stairs many times, passing out over a thousand sandwiches. The owner always gave me a soft drink and the latest news. Danny, the bartender, was saved after the first year and never went back to his old profession. In fact, many people were saved, but we always went back there to share soft drinks and the Good News with those who had never heard it or at least had never realized the Good News was meant for them.

A few months before they tore down the bar, we had a meeting with a power and light company vice president to see if our ministry could buy the bar and keep it open as a day shelter. We wanted a place where the homeless could be served soft drinks and sandwiches along with some Good News. He told me that he would allow it if he alone could make the decision. Unfortunately, he could not.

This may sound odd to you, but every time the hymn with the words "Jesus! what a Friend for sinners!" is played and sung in our church, I hear cracking pool balls, tinkling beer bottles, and creaking old stairs. I smell tuna. I consider afresh how our God is a redemptive God who is on the loose, seeking, searching, and saving. I see Danny and a host of smiling faces and a half-burned-out neon sign flashing on and off.

⹀11 The Father God Who Weeps

Oh, that my head were a spring of water and my eyes a fountain of tears! I would weep day and night for the slain of my people.
                                                                —JER. 9:1

The Father heart of God is a wonderful reality that has been written about often by gifted writers down through the ages. Mere words will never be able to fully describe the depth and expanse of God's love for His children.

Jeremiah is often called "the weeping prophet." Though Jeremiah's grief and pain were very real and very justified, it was the broken heart of God that he was attempting to portray. God's tears and Jeremiah's tears intermingled.

I witnessed a father's heartbreak one day. I was working part-time at a major hospital in order to make ends meet financially during the early days of my ministry. My position was titled "emergency room clerk." The basic duty of the job was to handle the abundance of paperwork an emergency room generates. Tragedies and sorrow were commonplace there. The very gifted medical staff was fairly adjusted to the daily trauma. I never became accustomed to it.

One summer morning a call came, informing us that the hospital helicopter was flying in a 12-year-old girl who had been struck by a car. I could tell by the tone of the doctor's voice that the child was in very serious condition.

The medical staff met the patient at the helipad and rushed her to the main trauma room. In just 20 minutes the commotion was over. Her injuries were beyond the lifesaving efforts of our finest trauma team.

Still shaken by the news of her death, I was sitting at the front desk of the emergency room when a man and a woman

32   *Doug Forsberg*

rushed in and approached me. I knew in an instant they were the girl's parents. I knew the truth, even though they did not. It was not my duty to inform family members of their loved one's condition, but it was my duty to lead them back to the "family room," where the doctor would meet them.

As emergency room clerk it was my job to acquire information about each patient, such as name, address, age, insurance, location of accident, and so on. I found the location of the accident from the police report. It was a familiar intersection that I drove by nearly every day.

I will never forget that little girl. I will also never be able to forget what I witnessed while driving home from work that night. While sitting in my car at a red light, I suddenly realized I was at the very intersection where the day's tragedy had taken place. It was a holy moment. The moment was made holier still when I noticed a man sitting on the bus stop bench by himself. He was sobbing uncontrollably. His face was buried in his hands, and the sleeves of his shirt were wet with tears. There were several cars at that intersection, and several people must have looked on in wonder at the lonely figure whose clothes were wet with tears. I alone knew the truth. He was the little girl's father, and his heart was broken.

If the Bible teaches us anything, it teaches us that the heart of God is breakable. It loves and cherishes, and it suffers loss. It yearns and desires and draws and longs. It breaks. God weeps. The reality of His heart's breaking can be clearly seen in the tear-soaked sleeves of Jeremiah, in the cries of Rachel over her children, in the deep sobs of a lonely figure at a bus stop, and in the Blood that dropped in a garden called Gethsemane and on a hill called Golgotha.

=12 Heroes

But when you give to the needy, do not let your left hand
know what your right hand is doing, so that your giving may
be in secret. Then your Father, who sees what is done in
secret, will reward you. —MATT. 6:3-4

In a forgotten downtown neighborhood in my hometown of
Kansas City stands a small, run-down grocery store called
Ruth's Confectionery. Famous people are never seen there.
Once in a while, however, you can spot a hero.

There are also heroes in the Bible. Men and women who
responded to God's call with courage, dignity, love, and faith
are numerous in the Scriptures.

It seems to me that the word *hero* is interchangeable between the secular world and the Christian world, because be-
lievers and nonbelievers all have heroes. A major difference,
however, can be seen in just who our heroes are. Secular heroes are easy to spot. They endorse shoes, hamburgers, hot
dogs, and beer. Their faces can be seen on billboards, bubble
gum cards, and cereal boxes. They write books, appear on talk
shows, and are almost always wealthy from the fame their
heroism has brought.

A Christlike hero is an entirely different story. Heroes for
Christ, for the most part, go unnoticed. Notice them and they
cringe. Reward them and they refuse. Praise them and they deny. Honor them and they question.

Someone once said that we must not lean on our heroes,
but they are wonderful for steadying ourselves when we have
lost our balance. I know many heroes. They serve and love without notice and are always there for me when I lose my balance.

In my opinion, the inner city needs more heroes—not the

Doug Forsberg

shoe-endorsing type, but the foot-washing type. Heroes like my friend Paul, who will be most angry with me for mentioning him here. Paul is a layman who works hard at his job, serves faithfully in his church, and is a tremendous father and husband to his family. That alone is heroic, I suppose, but the true heroism in this man, as is usually the case, goes unnoticed.

Paul's work takes him to various stores across the city. He distributes snack products and in so doing develops close friendships with all types of store managers. One of his stores is Ruth's Confectionery, located in an inner-urban area high in crime and low in morale. Ruth herself is poor, and yet, because of her kind heart, she allows her patrons to charge their groceries when money is lacking. Needless to say, several of Ruth's customers run up charges with no hope of repaying.

Paul discovered Ruth's problem of unpaid charge accounts one day while he was delivering snacks to her store. He asked to see the box that contained 3" x 5" cards showing the various accounts of her customers. Since that day, Paul goes down to Ruth's Confectionery and silently pays the debts of Ruth's customers.

One day while Paul was in Ruth's store paying other people's debts, a small boy came in to purchase a box of cereal. Paul paid for the cereal along with the other charges. After a lengthy explanation of what had just happened, the boy suddenly realized his $2 were no longer needed to purchase the cereal. He now had $2 to spend on anything he wanted in the store. Ruth and Paul watched the little boy, anticipating that he would probably purchase a candy bar or some pop. Instead, the boy bought milk. With a gleam in his eye and a smile on his face, he took the milk, saying, "Now, I can finally have some milk to go with my cereal!"

In a forgotten downtown neighborhood in my hometown of Kansas City stands a small, run-down grocery store called Ruth's Confectionery. Famous people are never seen there, but once in a while you can spot a hero.

=13 Faces

His face was like the sun shining in all its brilliance. —REV. 1:16

I found out a few years ago that I am a "summer." I learned it from the lady who cuts my hair. She revealed this profound discovery to me while casually clipping away at what hair I have left.

"What on earth is a 'summer'?" I asked.

She responded with a lengthy list of colors I should and should not wear. "Wear blue-based colors, not yellow-based colors, and never wear beige. Beige will bleach you right out!" I was wearing my favorite beige shirt at the time.

Staring at my own face in the mirror, I replied, "I came in here a happy-go-lucky guy. Now I find out I'm a balding, bleached-out 'summer'!"

As I left the Klipotiket (that was the name of the place—I think it means "expensive" in Swedish), she shouted one more piece of advice: "Wear soft pastels! They'll make you look glorious!"

Generally speaking, our country loves a glorious face. Men and women who are fortunate enough to be born beautiful can sell their faces to market products from cologne to pizza rolls. A glorious face can be worth millions and can bring a person world acclaim.

The value of faces overall has diminished. Maybe it's because the world crowd has become too large. Every one of us often feels like just "a face in the crowd." Maybe it's not so much the size of the crowd but the size of our hearts that has changed. Ads on television showing the faces of hungry children in the third world hardly affect us anymore. Commuter trains pass the ghettos of our country. I often wonder if the passengers notice the faces of the children playing in the streets.

Doug Forsberg

In Rev. 1:16, John describes Christ as having a face "like the sun shining in all its brilliance." Many times I have desired to see the face of God, to see with my own eyes a glimpse of that glorious, loving face. One day while playing baseball with some poor children of an unnoticed neighborhood, I thought I saw a reflection. In their little faces, dirty with street dust, I believe I saw a reflection of that face that notices and loves all faces.

Years ago I heard a man say that in the face of the poor you can see the face of God. I wondered then. I know now.

=14 Glory

And the glory of the Lord shone around them.   —LUKE 2:9

I will always remember my first inner-city Christmas. It was a time of hard work. It was also a time of wonder, awe, and learning. Some old words took on new meaning. One such word was the word *glory*.

Do you ever wonder if maybe we have allowed the world to step in and redefine some of our most precious words? In the age of Hollywood and Steven Spielberg, we have grown to expect the spectacular, the unimaginable, the dazzling, and the breathtaking. These words have nothing to do with glory. Glory is the presence of the Lord. Often His glory is found in the not so spectacular, the not so unimaginable, the not so dazzling, and the not so breathtaking. The lives of the poor who follow Christ are hardly spectacular, but often "the glory of the Lord" shines "round about them" (KJV).

The other day, while looking for some old pictures, I found the newsletter I mailed to our supporters during that first Christmas. The truth of it still remains a part of my heart:

Dear Friends,

This is a special Christmas for me this year. This is my first Christmas as a head pastor, and, of course, it is our first Christmas as a church. This being our first Christmas, I am sincerely attempting to help our people understand the true meaning of Christmas.

Imagination helps. It is hard to imagine angels singing "Glory to God in the highest" over a barn with a newborn baby lying in a trough. It's hard to imagine the King of Kings lying in swaddling clothes while mere shepherds look on.

As I have tried to spark their imagination to understand

                                      Doug Forsberg

the first Christmas and what it still means, something unexpected happened. I have discovered that the poor know more about Christmas than we middle class. We get caught up in trees and shopping and holiday plans. We buy manger scenes, tinsel, lights, neckties, and cologne. The poor, on the other hand, get caught up in the message. The glorious message that even if we live in a home that is no better than a barn, even if all we have are swaddling clothes and a teenage mother, somehow, someway, God is with us, and there are angels overhead.

The irony and wonder of this Christmas has been this: I came to these people with my master's degree and middle-class background, hoping to teach them the true meaning of Christmas. Instead, they taught me. Imagine that.

꞊15 Presence

God is present in the company of the righteous. —PS. 14:5

On the street everybody goes by his or her first name. And for the people who live there, their names are usually all they have to call their own. Most of the ones I met had nicknames such as "Buzz," "Cowboy," "Mr. B," "Willie," "Doc," and "Ivory," to name a few. All of them carried, along with their names, their own individual uniqueness and wisdom.

I can still remember Cowboy, Kevin, and Ivory. They would always be the first to arrive and the last to leave our street meetings. They were always there to lend a hand whenever needed and always free to offer advice even when it wasn't needed. The three of them taught me priceless lessons during those wonder years.

In the beginning, our ministry consisted of several cars full of hot dogs, iced tea, clothes, and Bibles. The street people would gather around the cars, and we would talk, eat, listen, and pray. Every night as we were packing up and preparing to head home, Cowboy, Kevin, and Ivory would come over. Each of them would shake our hands and repeat the same sentence: "Thanks for coming down." "Thanks for coming down." "Thanks for coming down."

It took me a year to fully understand that God was using Cowboy, Kevin, and Ivory to teach us a most treasured lesson. By simply saying "Thanks for coming down," they were expressing their gratitude for our greatest gift to them. It wasn't the food, the tea, the Bibles, or the clothes. It was our presence—the simple act of showing up.

It was difficult to find volunteers in those days. Everyone had a simple sentence to excuse himself or herself from assisting us in our ministry: "I wouldn't know what to say." "I wouldn't know what to do." "I'm not trained for that sort of ministry." "I don't feel called to the street people."

It was Cowboy, Kevin, and Ivory who taught us that a Christian's most powerful ministry tool is not training, or wisdom, or food, or clothes, though all of these are important. It is our presence, and the One whose presence we carry. Many of our most fruitful volunteers did not have training, education, personal resources, or a calling. They simply cared enough to "go down." That alone meant more to the likes of Cowboy, Kevin, and Ivory than anything.

Maybe what the world needs is His presence in us—and our presence in the world.

"Thanks for coming down."

⹀16 Standard Equipment

*When you give a reception, invite the poor, the crippled, the
lame, the blind, and you will be blessed, since they do not
have the means to repay you.* —LUKE 14:13-14, NASB

My friend Charles was one statistic of Dallas. In 1985 Mayor
Stark Taylor appointed a special committee on the homeless,
headed by Annette Strauss, who later became mayor herself,
and Harry Tanner of the city council. Their report was excellent
and well researched. It covered several issues surrounding
homelessness, including housing, the causes of homelessness,
health care needs among the homeless, and so on. The report
also gave some suggestions to alleviate the problems. It began
with a few statistics. All were tragic. Some were startling.

Three statistics were particularly alarming. The first dealt
with the sheer numbers of homeless people. In 1982 it was reported that the Salvation Army alone served 15,058 people. Of
those, 1,817 were children. Some estimated the total metroplex
homeless population at over 25,000.

The second startling statistic surrounded the health care
needs of homeless people. The Dallas County Department of
Health Services estimated that roughly 12 percent of the homeless population had tuberculosis, more than 10 times the ratio
found in the general population. Interviews with health pro-
viders to homeless people in downtown Dallas cited "high in-
cidences of upper respiratory problems including colds, em-
physema, bronchitis, pneumonia; infections, skin rashes, bites
from insects and rodents, scabies, lice, and nutritional problems."

The third tragic statistic involved my friend Charles. It
was reported in the mayor's study that approximately 30 per-

cent of the Dallas homeless population consisted of deinstitutionalized, mentally ill people. I personally witnessed the fact that these people were almost always kind and tenderhearted; yet, as a colleague described them, they lacked the "standard equipment" required to function in society.

In our country of rugged individualism and opportunity, it has been difficult for us to understand the plight of the homeless. Couldn't they just work their way off the streets? I was discussing the homeless problem with a Dallas businessman one day, and he responded like many of us did before we knew the truth: "Anyone can make it in this country if he or she is willing to work for it." He never realized that a great number of the homeless are children or mentally ill adults.

One Saturday night while we were feeding the homeless, Charles came over to where I was standing. A friend of his, Tony, walked beside him. They were both obviously excited about something. As they approached, Charles exclaimed, "We both got jobs!"

"That's great!" I replied.

"I'm going to sell balloons on the street, and my friend Tony here is going into the navy!" Charles said with excitement.

Later that night I asked Tony if he was looking forward to being a sailor. "Oh, yeah," he said. "I'm taking my aptitude test tomorrow." As we discussed the navy, I realized that he had not yet been accepted—he had just made some initial applications.

I knew Tony had trouble reading. I pointed to a bread wrapper on one of the folding tables. "Tony, what is this word?" I asked, while pointing to the word *bread*. Tony could not answer. Even though I encouraged him that night to take the test, Tony never joined the navy.

I had a discussion with Charles as well. "How much are the balloons that you are going to sell?" I asked.

"Fifty cents," he happily replied.

"That's a good price—you should sell lots of them," I said. "Do you want to practice some selling, Charles?" I asked.

"Sure!" he answered.

I asked him, "If a man buys one balloon and hands you a dollar, how much change would he get back?" All during the next hour Charles came up to me with different answers.

He never got it right.

=17 Grandmas

Even when I am old and gray, do not forsake me, O God, till I declare your power to the next generation, your might to all who are to come. —PS. 71:18

The true victims of inner-city poverty and violence are the children. Many times the true heroes are the grandmas.

We have discovered in many cases that the grandmothers are the ones who rise to the occasion of holding the family together. A large proportion of urban children are being raised by their grandmothers. Fathers are often absent for various reasons. The mothers are either working or are too young themselves to be competent in handling the pressures and decisions of urban motherhood. Often the total burden falls upon "Grandma."

My wife and I have personally witnessed grandmothers raising up to five or six children with courage, perseverance, and simple faith. These loving, hardworking women are hardly ever mentioned or noticed by society, and yet they are often holding the last few threads of the fabric of society together. On many Sundays I have welcomed new children to our church who when asked, "Who brought you to church today?" would smile and say, "Grandma."

I have tremendous respect for grandmas, because I was very fortunate to have two wonderful grandmothers. When one of them passed away during the Christmas season of 1984, my father and his brothers asked if I would officiate at the funeral. I was honored and accepted. I struggled over what to say to honor her. As I thought and prayed and asked God what to say, I believe He led me to a precious insight.

As I reflected on the beauty of my grandmother's life, I realized her beauty was very similar to the beauty of Christmas. Grandma was a simple woman who had a simple faith and lived in a simple little town. Is it not at Christmastime that we wonder at the beauty of the truth that when God gave us His most precious Gift, He entrusted that precious Gift into the hands of a simple woman who had a simple faith and lived in a simple little town? I think it was only proper that God took my grandma home at Christmastime.

My other grandma had passed away several years earlier, in 1971. During my childhood, my Grandma Turner lived with my family. She taught me my first in-depth lessons about Jesus. The early formation of my faith was lovingly constructed by her, the closest friend I ever had. Her smile, her laugh, her simple faith, and her singing will live with me always. A few years ago I wrote a poem about her. I share it here as a tribute to her and all the other grandmothers whose simple lives of loving continue to mold young hearts.

Grandma's Voice and Mom's Piano

In the springtime of my childhood,
  Long before I was a man,
When the hourglass of my life
  Had the top part full of sand,

I battled nearly every foe
  A young heart's sure to fight;
Fear of death, fear of pain,
  Fear of darkness with no light.

But at nighttime on my pillow
  When thoughts of fear were soon to start,
It was the sound of Grandma's singing
  That drove shadows from my heart.

Doug Forsberg

For down the stairs, across the room,
    Nearly every night,
Mom would play our old piano
    With Grandma at her right.

They would sing "The Rugged Cross"
    Of Jesus, "What a Friend"!
Grandma's voice and Mom's piano
    Beneath my room would always blend.

Rising up the stairway,
    Down the hall, into my room,
Songs of heaven, songs of Jesus,
    Always drove away the gloom.

Now the springtime of my childhood
    Has all but gone away.
Grandma's gone to be with Jesus,
    And Mom lives so far away.

But at nighttime on my pillow,
    When thoughts of fear are soon to start,
I can still hear the singing
    That once drove shadows from my heart.

Coming down the stairs of heaven,
    Down through time into my room,
Songs of heaven, songs of Jesus,
    Still drive away my gloom.

"The Old Rugged Cross" of Jesus,
    My Savior, "What a Friend"!
Grandma's voice and Mom's piano
    Will in my heart forever blend.

=18 Possessors of Heaven

Jesus said, "Let the little children come to me, and do not hinder them, for the kingdom of heaven belongs to such as these." —MATT. 19:14

When someone mentions the inner city, I do not think of poverty, crime, violence, or drugs. I think of kids. The inner cities of our country are teeming with children, and because of that one truth there is hope. Kids are impressionable. They can be taught to love and worship God. They can be taught to be kind and giving. The crucial question that confronts our country is simple: *Who is going to reach them first?*

What has made urban ministry so very enjoyable for my wife and me has been the kids. Their smiles, their laughter, and their hugs have sustained us through some very dark days. One day, when I was very seriously contemplating giving up, a child came up to me as I was getting into my car to drive home from the church office and hugged me. That one hug kept me going.

My mind recalls a thousand times when a child blessed us with humor or a sentence of truth that seemed as if heaven itself was guiding the statement.

One Sunday while I was preaching, I noticed a young girl around six or seven years of age sitting in the front pew. She was new to our church. She was staring at me during the whole sermon as if plagued by a curious thought. It was during the early days of my ministry, and my hair was quite a bit thicker then, and longer too. After the message I was greeting people in the back of the church when the little girl came up to me and spoke, revealing her curious thought. "You look like Jesus—but you sound like Kermit!"

Often our churches were the very first church some chil-

Doug Forsberg

dren had ever attended. These precious kids knew nothing of church behavior and protocol. This made for some very exciting and eventful worship services.

One Sunday morning, Rance, a freckle-faced, red-haired boy with a purple earring, was sitting in the service. In the middle of the service, he raised his hand and asked a question many of us have desired to ask our pastor: "How long we goin' ta haf ta sit here anyway?"

One Saturday afternoon we took several kids to the zoo. We were carpooling, and the backseat of my car held three boys, ages three, four, and six. When we arrived at the zoo, it was my blessing to find that the six-year-old had eaten almost all the Oreos, the four-year-old had spilled the soda pop, and the three-year-old had wet his britches. As I helped them out and surveyed the big stain on my car seat, the pop puddle, and the Oreo crumbs, the six-year-old looked up at me with black bits of Oreo on his face and teeth and asked, "Are you mad, Rever Doug?" How could I be?

My wife, DeVonna, and I were married in my first pastorate. I had planted the church in Fort Worth while I was single, and it was a special event for the pastor to be married in his own church. We had a great ceremony, complete with 12 inner-city children whom we loved dearly. Each one wore the best clothes he or she owned. Even so, some of the boys wore kneeless jeans and faded sweaters.

After the ceremony, my mother was talking with Robert, an eight-year-old boy who had been in our wedding. He told my mother that he had been to weddings before, but "This was the first I ever 'peticipated' in." I told my mom later, as we were laughing over his statement, that Robert was special. When he had first come to our church, his entire family was hooked on cocaine, even him. Now, after being delivered from it, he was free once again to be a kid.

During our first Christmas as man and wife, DeVonna headed up our children's Christmas play. It was wonderful. Thirty children acted out the Christmas story. I watched it for the first time along with the congregation on the Sunday before Christmas. Joseph was black, Mary was white, and Baby Jesus was a real baby. The angels were Hispanic, and the shepherds were multitudinous—and all under the age of five. After the pageant I asked one of the boys who he had been in the play. He looked up at me and said proudly, "I was King Arthur!"

The plight of the inner cities is often a topic of heated political debate, often the main story in the newspaper, often a tragic story on the news. The next time you hear about the inner city, read about "the ghetto," or drive by or near "the bad part of town," please remember this: It is home to a great many precious and impressionable children who happen to possess "the kingdom of heaven."

Doug Forsberg

=19 My Little Shadow

I praise you, Father, Lord of heaven and earth, because you have hidden these things from the wise and learned, and revealed them to little children. —MATT. 11:25

Ralphie died in the summer of 1991. He was 10 years old. All children are special, and all children add joy to the lives of those they love, but to me, his pastor, Ralphie was beyond special.

I first met Ralphie when he was 9. He came to our Saturday children's ministry, which we called "Kids' Klub." It met in our church's large parking lot and provided the children with games, sports, activities, crafts, special guests, and lunch. An average Kids' Klub would have around 65 children attending. From the first time Ralphie came to Kids' Klub until the week God took him home, he never missed Kids' Club or Sunday School.

It's common teaching in most seminaries that pastors should not have favorites, nor should they get too close to any one of their parishioners. The magnetic joy that Ralphie brought to my life caused me unashamedly to break that rule. Everyone knew he was my favorite, and no one blamed me for selecting him. Those who knew Ralphie understood.

Every Saturday morning when I pulled into my parking spot at the church, there was a somewhat plump, freckle-faced, red-haired boy with a smile as big as all outdoors to greet me. He would open my car door and greet me with a hug. "Can I be your helper today, Pastor Doug?"

"Sure you can, Ralphie. You're the best helper a pastor ever had."

What I loved most was just to watch his happiness. Happiness followed Ralphie like the cloud of dust that followed

Pigpen in the Peanuts cartoon. If you got too close, his joy would rub off.

At home, at school, at church, at Kids' Klub, Ralphie was a joy bringer and a peacemaker. His principal and teachers informed me later that if there was fighting or conflict at school, Ralphie was there making peace and seeing to it that no one was harmed, sometimes even endangering himself.

The last Sunday of his life I had the children come forward in our worship service for the customary "Pastor Doug blessing" before I dismissed them for children's church. While I prayed that day, Ralphie had his arms around me so tightly I could hardly take a breath to say my prayer.

The next day I drove nine of our children to Leesburg, Florida, for our District Children's Camp. Eight of the kids had paid their own way. Ralphie was unable to pay, so DeVonna and I paid his way. He had never been to camp, and for the month prior he had asked me 100 questions: "Will we fish?" "Will we swim?" "Will we go hiking?" "How often do we eat?"

I drove the church van home after making sure everyone was settled. Ralphie was to stay in the "House of Noah" cabin.

Pastors receive many phone calls each day. Every so often the phone rings with some news that suddenly reminds him that his heart is all too human and capable of being shattered. I knew that maybe someday such a call would come, but no preparation can be made for the tragic phone calls of life—and death.

Ralphie had drowned in the swimming pool his first night at camp. He had squeezed under the high fence while the pool was unattended. He jumped in and woke up in heaven. They found his body at 8:30 P.M. My phone rang at 9:00.

Kids' Klub was never again quite the same for me. My little shadow was gone. No little freckle-faced boy was there to open up my car door and ask, "Can I be your helper today, Pastor Doug?" For several Saturdays I would slip into my office alone and weep. It was the price I paid for breaking the "Don't get too close" rule.

The Saturday after Ralphie's death, the 60 or so kids gath-

Doug Forsberg

ered for Kids' Klub. We had hardly started before Virakone, one of our Vietnamese children, asked, "Where's Ralphie?" Suddenly all eyes were fixed upon me, waiting for an answer. Vietnamese, Cambodian, Laotian, Thai, Korean, Hispanic, Afro-American, and Caucasian kids were all wondering where Ralphie was. He had been a friend to them all. With all the courage I could muster, I told them the truth.

The grief of all of us who loved him has been very deep. Deeper still is the sweet assurance that Jesus, whom Ralphie loved dearly, loved him as well. Now Christ himself is the divine Recipient of that precious smile. Now He must answer that tender question: "Can I be Your helper today?"

=20 82,000 Silent Children

Now this was the sin of your sister Sodom: She and her daughters were arrogant, overfed and unconcerned; they did not help the poor and needy. —EZEK. 16:49

In the summer of 1972 my hometown of Kansas City was anxiously awaiting the opening of our new Harry S. Truman Sports Complex, which was to harbor the world's only side-by-side stadiums: Arrowhead Stadium for football and Royals Stadium for baseball. As August approached, I longed to attend that very first game in Arrowhead, the home of our Kansas City Chiefs. For a teenager who loved sports, attending that first game would be the thrill of a young lifetime.

I was fortunate to have been granted the thrill of attending that first game. My father had ordered tickets for that Saturday night preseason game well in advance. The tickets arrived in the mail just a week or so before the big game.

I do not recall very many details of that first Arrowhead game. What I do remember vividly was the size of the crowd and my father's reaction to it. Neither my father nor I had ever been in a crowd of 82,000 people. All evening during that memorable game Dad kept saying, "Wow—would you look at all the people!"

Eight years later I was a student at Nazarene Theological Seminary in Kansas City. While working in the library on a research paper, I held a copy of *Newsweek* dated February 18, 1980. In that magazine was an appalling article on world hunger. The article cited a tragic truth about our world: In 1980 over 30 million children would die of hunger-related illness. Overwhelmed by that staggering figure, I took a sheet of paper and divided 30 million by 365. I desired to know how many children would die each day.

The answer was roughly 82,000. My mind suddenly recalled that evening when Dad and I had sat in a crowd of 82,000 people. I heard once again those words my dad kept repeating on that warm Missouri evening: "Wow—would you look at all the people!"

On a winter afternoon in 1980 while I was studying in the seminary library, a tender memory of my youth was transformed into a tragic thought: Arrowhead Stadium and 82,000 silent children. That thought haunts me still.

⹀21 Piercing the Barrier

There is no fear in love. But perfect love drives out fear.

—1 JOHN 4:18

It is one of humanity's strongest enemies. When it comes to inner-city ministry, it is one of Christianity's greatest foes. This enemy is fear. The barrier of fear surrounds every ghetto, intimidating any would-be healer. It is thicker than any iron curtain. It is darker than despair itself and more imposing than an army. If there is to be a new dawn of hope for America's troubled cities, we must first remove our fear. If there is to be healing and revival, there must first be courage. The battle for our cities will not be fought in the streets or in the halls of Congress. It will be fought in our own individual hearts, for that is where fear resides. It is in our hearts where courage must conquer.

My own battle with fear was an intense and very personal one. Maybe it was my own experience of what the early mystics called "the dark night of the soul." I cannot report that I won the battle or that I do not fight the same battle still, but I can report that it was won *for* me.

In my own heart, fear was conquered, not by my courage, but by God's love. Once I understood, or I should say *began* to understand, the depth of God's love for me as a person and for those He had called me to, the fears began to crumble. Rising up from the rubble of fear came a faint glimmer of courage. This courage rested, not on my own strength to overcome, but on His strength to love. His love defeated my fear. His love brought to my heart the courage that must necessarily exist if we are ever to love others. We do indeed love "because he first loved us" (1 John 4:19).

One night I was sitting on a bus stop bench in the center

of downtown Dallas around 1 A.M. The streets were nearly deserted. I had been conversing with a homeless person for nearly two hours. The tall buildings surrounding us formed a sort of canyon, and only a sliver of sky was visible, but in that sliver of sky a star could be seen. I said to my homeless friend, "You know, the city's lights are so bright that a person hardly ever sees a star down here. Once in a while, though, a star outshines the city—like that one up there."

"Sure is a bright one," he replied, with eyes fixed.

God's love can outshine our fears much the same way as some stars can outshine the lights of a city.

=22 There Were Soldiers on the Corner

The written notice of the charge against him read: THE KING OF THE JEWS.
—MARK 15:26

When I was 10 years old my parents refused to allow me to go to the birthday party of my best friend. Larry and I were close. At school we played, laughed, ate, and studied together. I walked to school. Larry rode the bus. I lived in "the good part of town." Larry lived in "the bad part of town." Larry was Afro-American.

Twenty-five years ago, Larry made a statement to me. Even though we were only 10, I can still recall the passion, the love, and the hate of his words.

His statement came on a beautiful spring day in early April. It was a day, however, when my childhood would be pierced with adult realities. Walking to school that day, I felt an unfamiliar fear. There were soldiers on the corner. It was the day after the death of Martin Luther King Jr.

As Larry approached me in the hall that day, there was a barrier between us that our 10-year-old eyes had never before seen and that our young hearts had never before felt. Our childhood friendship had been interrupted in the same way an alarm clock interrupts a sweet dream. The pain of the centuries was in his eyes, and to some degree in mine as well. As we stood before each other in the hallway of Marlborough Elementary School on Friday, April 5, 1968, Larry said to me, "I love you, Doug, but I hate white people."

Demond is 10 years old. He lives in a small house in St. Petersburg, Florida. He attended our church while we pastored

Doug Forsberg

there. Demond is Afro-American and always reminded me of Larry, my childhood friend who loved me and whose birthday party I never got to attend. I often told the kids in our church that I loved them. For some reason, I spoke those words to Demond more often, saying to him what I wanted to say to Larry.

On the day Jesus died there were soldiers on the corner. They hated Him because He was a Jew.

Prejudice pierced Him then. Prejudice pierces Him still.

=23 What's in a Building?

But I say to you, that something greater than the temple is here.   —MATT. 12:6, NASB

When our church in Fort Worth was about a year and a half old, the church building we were worshiping in was sold. Our church, Riverside Community, had been leasing the fellowship hall. Suddenly, with only two weeks notice, we were homeless.

The congregation, around 75 people at the time, and I learned some priceless lessons in those two weeks. During the middle Sunday of those two eventful weeks, we worshiped outdoors in a nearby park. Seated on folding chairs on an outdoor basketball court, we discovered that God was as close to us then as He had been in our comfortable fellowship hall, maybe even closer. The beautiful outdoors and the sense of knowing that we were totally dependent upon Him and His weather gave our worship great meaning on that homeless Sunday. Brick and mortar do not a church make.

The next Sunday we had a new church home lovingly provided by the many caring people from the West Texas District of our denomination and our leader, Gene Fuller. It was an old building, but to us our new home was the most beautiful church building in the world. It was spacious, it had a big backyard, and it was ours. God had provided, as we knew He would.

As I was looking through some old pictures the other day, my heart was warmed to see a picture of that old building. While I pastored there, it never had heat or air conditioning. It had only one toilet, which overflowed often. It was home to a great many of God's smaller creatures. The foundation had sunk on one side, causing several of the rooms, including my

Doug Forsberg

office, to lean. Whenever a friend would drop by to visit my office for the first time, I would sing "Leaning on the Everlasting Arms," to their amusement and mine.

Our church building never really had beauty or grace or any of the fine appointments a church building is supposed to have. But that old building was a dear and precious place. In that building the poor heard the gospel, people were fed (we had dinner every Sunday), children laughed, and people were born into the Kingdom. In the winter we froze, in the summer we sweltered, but we always had a crowd. Newcomers often commented on how the Lord's tender presence had touched them. Everyone was welcome.

It was, of course, the loving people and the God they worshiped who made that place special. That feeling, however, seemed even more tender in those humble surroundings.

My wife and I were married in that leaning little church. Our marriage got off to a great start—because it was born in such a holy place.

=24 Cambodian Buddy

Go and make disciples of all nations. —MATT. 28:19

During the first week of our pastorate in St. Petersburg, I had the privilege of filling out the pastor's report for the previous year. The pastor before me had left good records, but even so, the job was laborious. Halfway through the report I decided to take a stroll through our new mission field to the corner grocery store for a bottle of soda. I decided to take the alley for the three-block walk.

As I strolled down the alley, I was amazed at the number of children. Their dark little faces were covered with dusty Florida soil. Their eyes, as large as saucers, watched my every move as I passed. Many of them ran or stepped aside to allow this white stranger through. These children, who were soon to become my friends, were Southeast Asian. Their ethnic backgrounds were Cambodian, Vietnamese, Thai, and Laotian. I smiled. They seemed to fear me.

A year later I was sitting in my office hard at work at the same tedious task of filling out my pastor's report. Halfway through I realized it had been a year since I took my first journey through the neighborhood. I decided to take the same walk. By this time our Kids' Klub ministry had begun, and now many of the children who were strangers the year before were my little buddies.

The first year my walk took about 25 minutes. The second year it took about two hours. As I headed down that dusty alley, the kids came running. "Pastor Duck!" "Kids' Klub today?" "Pastor Duck, can you play?" When I arrived back at my office, my shirt was ruined. It was stretched, torn, and dirt-stained. Some of the kids had hugged me after eating peanut

Doug Forsberg

butter and jelly sandwiches. When I arrived home later that day, my wife asked, "What in the world happened to you?" "What a difference a year makes!" I said, smiling.

One of those little buddies of mine was Sori. He was five or six and had a broad, heartwarming, toothless smile. Sori was my mail buddy. He would ride his little bicycle to the church on warm, sunny afternoons around three o'clock. I would come out of the church, open our mailbox, and read the mail while seated next to Sori on our church steps. While his little face beamed, I would hand him our junk mail. Catalogs, advertisements, you name it—he received them all with joy. Receiving my gifts of unwanted mail seemed to make him proud I had chosen him for such honor.

One day Sori and I were sitting on our church steps. There hadn't been much mail that day, and we were sitting there in silence, just soaking up the sun. Sori never said much. English was still fairly difficult for him. While sitting there next to my little Cambodian buddy, I marveled at our differences. Age, ethnicity, language, culture—we were different in every way. I also marveled at how a man from Kansas City could be seated next to a boy from Cambodia on church steps in Florida. Yet there we sat, side by side—as buddies.

Church steps have a way of bringing people together. Maybe they, too, are sacred.

=25 Passionate Struggler

Who shall deliver me from the body of this death?

—ROM. 7:24, KJV

Richard was a kind man who struggled most of his life. His struggle finally ended in the summer of 1990 when he died from an AIDS-related illness. Richard was a caring person who came to our church, looking for hope and victory over his struggle. I would like to believe he found the hope and victory for which he longed. I do know for sure that he gave more than he received.

Writing as a man who has spent more than seven years in Christian institutions preparing for the ministry, I look back upon my education with a certain degree of sorrow. My sorrow is essentially simple in origin: I learned the correct answers long before I had mastered the questions.

When Richard entered our church and our lives, he arrived with his own intense struggle and set of questions. Quite frankly, I did not know how to deal with him at first or how to answer him. The struggle with homosexuality began for him at an early age. Shackled by a deep loneliness and an agonizing shame, he fought his tragic battle into adulthood. Protecting people from his true self, he lived an exemplary Christian life until the day he resolved within himself that his struggle could never be won. By the time he came to us, he was HIV-positive and wrestling with a deep bitterness toward the Church.

It was Richard who helped me realize that during my formal Christian education, people had become topics to me. Homosexuals, the poor, the outcast were mere topics over which we students would conduct theological debate. When homosexuals, the poor, and the outcast became my friends, suddenly

Doug Forsberg

I was no longer a defender of a position but a colaborer in their struggle. What was once their struggle became my struggle.

Now, whenever AIDS or homosexuality is discussed or debated, I find myself becoming strangely silent. I recall Richard's face and the prayers that he prayed. I remember his kindness and his love for people, for animals, and for life itself. I remember his intense desire to please Christ and his intense fear of having failed Him. I remember his hope that someday the Church would come to see homosexuals, not as topics for debate, but as people to love.

On the day Richard died, I lost a very close friend. He was mourned by all who knew him, not because he won his struggle, but because he fought it so bravely, openly, honestly, and with a deep love and affection for the Redeemer that "strugglers" truly know.

ᵈ26 The Unborn Poor

Is not this the kind of fasting I have chosen: to loose the chains of injustice and untie the cords of the yoke, to set the oppressed free and break every yoke? Is it not to share your food with the hungry and to provide the poor wanderer with shelter—when you see the naked, to clothe him, and not to turn away from your own flesh and blood? —ISA. 58:6-7

She was about four weeks old when I dedicated her in our Sunday morning worship service. Her name is Emily. With her parents standing beside me, I prayed the prayer of dedication in a service that seemed illuminated by God's Spirit and Emily's bright eyes and heart-melting smile. I cry easily to begin with, but as I began my prayer that day, I knew I was a goner.

Several months before Emily was born, her parents made an appointment to meet with me. When they stepped into my office, I could immediately sense they were very troubled. I braced myself for bad news. "I'm pregnant," the woman said as they both sat despairingly on the couch.

"That's wonderful!" I responded. I then questioned them as to why there was no joy in their news.

Their answer was simple: "We just cannot afford another child, and we are considering an abortion."

During our years of pastoral ministry, my wife and I counseled various couples who were confronted with this very dilemma. We soon learned that though many women in our country abort their babies for various reasons, the poor struggle with the economic future and often suffer anguish over what they view as a tragic choice between abortion or a life of poverty. To them, either decision is a heartbreaking one.

I am happy to report that no couple we counseled ever

Doug Forsberg

aborted their baby. Their decision to have their baby rested not only on the Scriptures' teaching of the sanctity of life but also on its implication that God too cries easily, especially when little ones like Emily are being offered to His service. "And my God will meet all your needs according to his glorious riches in Christ Jesus" (Phil. 4:19). That was Emily's verse.

I learned early that there is a tremendous price to be paid if one desires to preach that all life is sacred. For not only does life begin at conception, but responsibility as well. Emily now sits at her parents' table, but in the scriptural sense she is seated at my table as well.

On that teary and joyful day of Emily's dedication, I quoted her verse. I also quoted, "For I was hungry and you gave me something to eat, I was thirsty and you gave me something to drink, I was a stranger and you invited me in, I needed clothes and you clothed me, I was sick and you looked after me" (Matt. 25:35-36). Those verses belonged to me.

=27 It Lasts! It Lasts!

And the ransomed of the LORD will return. They will enter Zion with singing; everlasting joy will crown their heads. Gladness and joy will overtake them, and sorrow and sighing will flee away. —ISA. 35:10

His home was an apartment the size of a small garage. His clothes were a bit ragged and out of style. He lived alone and rode the bus to the grocery store. He walked slowly yet deliberately with a cane. On his 90th birthday he received 1,500 birthday cards. Leon was the most joyful person I have ever met.

Leon was not just a servant of God, but a lover of God as well. He lived his life as a schoolteacher, and even in his old age he could still remember many of his students. They in turn remembered him. On Leon's 90th birthday in 1989, the mailman came to him with a bag on a cart, full of loving letters to Professor Edmiston. That mailbag was a tribute of love the likes of which is rarely seen. After reading every card, Leon donated them to our church's World Mission Division, to be used again for missionaries. That was Leon's style: smiling, laughing, telling stories, quoting puns, and, of course—giving.

Every Wednesday morning for two years I picked Leon up at 9:15 A.M., and both of us traveled to the nearby nursing home, where we conducted the midweek worship service. I played the organ, and we sang our favorite old hymns. I gave a short devotional. It was Leon, however, who was the encourager. He laughed and joked with everyone as he passed out the hymnals. Within the span of 10 minutes, he had the receptionist, the nurses, the food service workers, and the residents all in smiles. Nursing homes can become gloomy places if left unministered to, but give it a Leon, and the place will light up.

Doug Forsberg

On a sunny Florida morning in the summer of 1993, I drove to the nursing home. This time I traveled alone. I cried the whole way and nearly had an accident. When I arrived, I walked down that familiar hall. The receptionist, the nurses, the food service workers, the activities director, and the residents all asked, "Where's Leon?" I assembled them all in the meeting room, cleared my throat, and said, "Leon is in heaven today. Last Thursday while he was eating breakfast and reading his morning paper, God took our Leon home." I continued to hold their midweek service for another year, but I was never able to make them smile the way Leon did.

One day a few years back, Leon gave his testimony at the nursing home for the first time. Before him was a rather strange mix of people. Some were young, and some were older than he. Most were in wheelchairs. Some were turning up their hearing aids. All were listening. Leon told them how he had been saved as a child. He told them of the death of his father, his mother, his wife. He told them of an illness he battled as a youth and how the doctors told him he would never see his 21st birthday. The thing I remember most was his telling them about the joy he had when he gave his heart to Jesus. Then with that sweet manner of his, he shouted so even the hard of hearing could hear him: "It lasts! It lasts! The joy lasts! The joy of the Lord is everlasting!"

He never lost that joy, even up to the young and tender age of 93.

=28 On the Fragile Wings of Hope

And hope does not disappoint us, because God has poured out his love into our hearts by the Holy Spirit, whom he has given us. —ROM. 5:5

After spending the past eight years of my life serving Christ in the inner city, I must readily admit that I have been given far more than I gave. I began as a young man who desired to teach and bless and give grace. I soon learned that I was the student, the recipient of blessing, and the one who was in need of grace. Ralphie, Richard, Leon, Sori, Emily, and all the other people God gave me the privilege to serve became my ministers.

I have learned that the inner city is a key arena of God's working. The love and hope of God abides in such strong measure there. Strangely enough, I have a certain degree of pity for suburban Christians who have never had the privilege to serve in this special area.

I have also learned that God makes choices. One such choice God made long ago was stated by James: "Has not God chosen those who are poor in the eyes of the world to be rich in faith and to inherit the kingdom he promised those who love him?" (2:5). I have personally witnessed this wealth and am the richer for it.

I thank God for His classrooms of grace. The Dallas junkyard, the street, Kids' Klub, the Palace of Dallas, the nursing homes—these were the classrooms where God taught me that His love is far-reaching, His hope is not disappointing, and though sin abounds, His grace does much more abound.

If there is hope for our inner cities, it must come from the likes of us. It is true that the government gives grant money for food, housing, education, and so on. It does not give out a dime

Doug Forsberg

for the advancement of God's kingdom or the teaching of the holiness ethic, nor does it provide workers for such efforts. These efforts must be funded and administered by us, ordinary people who long to show others the love and grace that we ourselves have found in Christ. May God grant us the courage, and may He reassure us that though the wings of hope are indeed fragile, because of Him they are strong enough to carry us all.

DATE DUE

Demco, Inc. 38-293